Reflections Of A Man

MR. AMARI SOUL

Reflections
Of A Man

Black Castle Media Group

First Edition

Cover Design by: BCMG Studios

Cover Photography by: Brandon Harris Photography

Library of Congress Cataloging-in-Publication Data has been applied for.

Paperback Edition	ISBN 978-0-9861647-0-5
Kindle Edition	ISBN 978-0-9861647-1-2
EPUB Edition	ISBN 978-0-9861647-2-9
Hardback Limited Edition	ISBN 978-0-9861647-3-6

This book is dedicated to my mother.
My greatest example of what a good woman is.

CONTENTS

CHAPTERS
PART I - FOR YOU

CHAPTERS

PART II - FOR HIM

PART III - FOR BOTH OF YOU

PART IV - MY PERSONAL COLLECTION

www.mramarisoul.com
www.facebook.com/mr.amarisoul
www.instagram.com/mr.amarisoul
www.twitter.com/mramarisoul
www.pinterest.com/mramarisoul

Introduction

Thank you for purchasing "Reflections Of A Man." It is my sincere hope that this book will be used by both men and women to enhance the quality of their personal relationships.

To the women, I hope this book encourages you to recognize the true value of your love, to reevaluate your standards, and to make the decision that you will no longer settle for anything less than someone who loves you, respects you, and truly makes you happy.

To the men, I hope this book will not only encourage you to want to learn more about the emotional needs of a woman, but that it will provide you with clear insight into what a woman truly needs from you, emotionally, to be happy.

I believe this book creates a true win-win situation for both men and women. On one hand, women gain a new perspective on the true value of their love, raise their standards, and refuse to settle. On the other hand, men become better equipped to, not only understand a woman's emotional needs, but they are better able to meet or exceed their new standards as well.

-Mr. Amari Soul

Part I
For You

CHAPTER

MAN FACTS

"There is no such thing as a self-made man; that's just an example of a man too caught up in himself to look around and acknowledge the strength of the woman standing next to him."

What Men Know

*"Most men know exactly what it would take to make
their woman happy. They're just too stubborn, too
egotistical or too lazy to do it."*

I believe most women, who have been with their man for any reasonable amount of time, want their man to know exactly what it would take to keep them happy. You drop subtle hints, you outright say it, and when you don't, it still comes across through your actions and reactions. So, for the most part, he should know. If he knows and still doesn't do it, it's most likely because of one of the previously mentioned reasons. If after all this time he still doesn't know, he simply hasn't been paying any attention to you at all.

A Man's Ego

"What's more fragile than a woman's heart?
A man's ego."

L et me explain. When you first meet a man and he lies to you about what his economic status is or what his current relationship status is, that's all to protect his ego. You see, at that point, he's decided that he's interested in you, but his insecurities are telling him that you won't accept him for who or what he is. So, he creates an illusion of who he thinks you would like him to be, thus reducing his chances of rejection. However, when you look a little deeper, it's not the rejection alone that he fears most. What he fears the most is the feeling that rejection causes and how that feeling impacts his ego. That is, in fact, his worst fear.

In the end, some men would be willing to go to any

lengths to protect their egos, up to and including lying to you, cheating on you, and ultimately breaking your heart.

When He Changes Around His Friends

"If he changes the way he treats you when he's around his friends, he either hasn't been keeping it real with them or he hasn't been keeping it real with you."

True love remains consistent regardless of the situation or the environment. If he truly loves you, his actions should show it whether you are in private, public, or the company of his friends. In fact, when he is around his friends, he should feel a heightened sense of pride just having you there with him. If he doesn't, it could mean he cares more about impressing his friends than he cares about how you feel. It's also possible that he's been lying to them all along about how he feels about you, or maybe he's been lying to you.

If He Doesn't Include You

❦

"A man who doesn't include you when he talks about his future, either isn't paying attention or he doesn't see you as being a part of it."

S ometimes, the best way to get an honest answer is not to ask the question directly but indirectly. If you have been with your man, for a reasonable amount of time, and you are unsure about what his intentions are regarding your future, ask him the following question: If you could paint a picture of how your life will be in five years, how would it look?

He should then begin to describe to you how, in his mind's eye, he envisions his life to look in five years.

You'll notice that he'll talk to you about all the things that are his primary focus; you would hope that you and the relationship would be one of them. Pay particularly close attention to how often he uses the word "me" or "I" instead of "us" or "we."

By the end of the conversation, you should have a pretty good idea of where you stand. The beautiful thing about it is he most likely won't even realize that he will have answered the big question that you never even asked.

Relationship Title
My "Main"

"Contrary to popular belief, this is not a compliment."

If he calls you his "main," that is not a compliment. What he is essentially saying to you is that you are not the only one. Nine times out of 10, if he calls you his "main," he has given all the other women he is seeing the same title as well.

In short, "my main" is a polite way of him telling you that he likes you enough to sleep with you but not enough to commit to you.

Self-Fulfilled Prophecy

"Some men have so convinced themselves that a good woman does not exist that they subconsciously will ruin a relationship, with a good woman, just to prove themselves right."

If his negative expectations about you are strong enough, those feelings will begin to manifest themselves in his actions. Eventually, this will cause him to act in a manner that will ultimately increase the chances of those negative expectations being fulfilled.

Is He Really "Willing To Wait?"

When a man says that he's willing to wait until you're ready, it doesn't necessarily mean he's willing to "wait."

Here is where the game changes. Now, to be fair, some men will honor that statement and not be intimate with anyone else during this "waiting period." However, those aren't the men I'm referring to here. The ones I'm referring to have a different plan in mind. What they plan to do is exactly what they said they would do, "wait until you are ready." The problem is the "waiting" is tied directly to you and only you, no one else. In short, he's agreed to not push the issue with you, thus earning brownie points for appearing not to be only after one thing.

In your mind, over the next few months, you're thinking he's really into you when, in fact, he's just biding his time until you're ready to give him what he wants. Meanwhile, his "side" is taking care of all the needs that you've decided not to provide. You see, it's easy for him to pass on dinner when he's been snacking all day.

So, don't be fooled. When a man tells you he's willing to "wait," clarify what he means and hold him to it. Also, during the waiting period, keep your eyes open for any subsequent changes in his pattern of behavior. Things like him not coming to see you or not calling you as often should peak your interest. Additionally, him disappearing for hours at a time with excuses like "I left my phone" or "my battery died" should be warning signs as well.

Above all, trust your intuition; it will tell you what you need to hear and not necessarily what you want to hear.

Is He Complaining About Your Standards?

❧

"When a man complains of your standards being too high, it is usually because he's used to dealing with women who have none."

Some men have gotten so used to dealing with women who have no standards that once they meet a woman who does, they don't know how to make the necessary adjustments. Instead of raising their level of performance, they complain in hopes that you will lower your standards, thus making it easier for them to appear to be good for you.

My advice is that you should never lower your standards to accommodate any man! If he is not capable of meeting or exceeding the standards that you have set, he's probably not the right man for you.

Eye Contact

"A man that won't look you in the eyes, either isn't interested in how you actually feel about the conversation, has confidence issues, or is hiding something from you."

Eye contact for a man is very important. It is one of the ways we establish ourselves during our interactions; it's how we convey a sincerity and seriousness that cannot be expressed any other way. So, for a man to avoid eye contact, it simply goes against our nature. I can only think of a few reasons as to why a man would avoid eye contact: (1) he is disregarding you, (2) he has confidence issues, (3) he's hiding something from you, or (4) he's simply lying to you. Either way, none of these qualities would do you well in your relationship.

The 4-Digit Passcode

"The answers to all your questions are not protected by his many lies, but rather by a tiny glass screen and a 4-digit passcode."

I'm just going to put it out there. I know, you'll get the old "if you trusted me, you wouldn't need to look at my phone" speech; I've been there, done that and it worked like a charm.

That statement is designed to make you feel guilty about asking him to confirm something that he should not have a problem confirming in the first place.

In a relationship, you two should be on the same page. If you can't see what he sees and he can't see what you see, chances are, you two are probably not on the same page. To be honest, you two might not even be in the same book!

As a side note, let me leave you with this: If you two can share the same house, the same bed, and the same bank account, how come he can't share his passcode?

Ultimatums Rarely Work

"When a man tells you that he is not ready to commit, believe him the first time. You can't convince him that he is ready. You will only be fooling yourself."

If you ever find yourself in the following situation, stop for a minute and think...

You are dating a man and you want things to move to the next level (commitment); however, he says he's not ready yet. You then tell him if he can't commit, you're moving on. If he comes right back and says, "Okay, I'm ready to commit," be careful. He's still not ready to commit to you; he just doesn't want to lose you or see you committed to someone else.

Any time a man agrees to a commitment after being given an ultimatum, be leery. He was honest in the beginning, but now he feels like he will lose you if he doesn't say what you want to hear. That's not the kind of commitment you want. You want it to be a decision he makes for himself because he wants it and not one where he feels like he was forced into making it.

In the end, ultimatums may get you what you want in the short term, but as time passes you'll see that he can't keep up the act forever. Slowly but surely you'll begin to realize that you may have changed his words, but he never changed his mind...now what?

When He Stops Doing The Small Things

"When he texts you, he's thinking about you.
When he calls you, he misses you.
When he shows up, he wants you.
When he suddenly stops doing all of the above for you,
he's doing it for someone else."

His Fear Of Being Hurt

"Sometimes, the problem isn't that he cannot give you love, the problem lies in his inability to let go of the fear of being hurt long enough to accept your love."

Think about this for a moment; when you give love, you control how you feel about it; when you're on the receiving end of love, those emotions are much harder to control. That's how you find yourself falling in love with someone without ever intending to do so.

For some men, they're fine as long as they're giving love. That's because they control that feeling. However, when you start to give it back and he begins to feel like he is losing that control, sometimes he will back away, out of the fear of being hurt. Not because he doesn't care for you, but because the feeling of being vulnerable and not in control of his feelings scares him.

Selfish Versus Selfless Man

"A selfish man would rather you be unhappy with him than to see you happy with someone else; however, a man who loves you selflessly, he'll set you free. Not in hopes that you would someday come back, but in hopes you would be found by a man that could be all the things he couldn't be."

NOTES:

_____

_____

_____

_____

_____

_____

_____

_____

_____

_____

CHAPTER

THE WRONG MAN

He could be a "good man" and still not be the
"right man" for you.

〰️◯〰️

How Could Someone So Right, Be So Wrong?

*"He could have the right face, the right smile, with the
right job, making the right amount of money,
but if he doesn't love and respect you,
he's still the wrong man for you."*

Make sure when you decide to give a man your time, you're doing it for the right reasons. Just because he looks nice or drives a nice car, doesn't mean anything if he disrespects you and treats you like you don't even exist. You have to be able to look past the superficial things and focus on "who he is" rather than "what he is" or "what he has." Otherwise, you might find yourself with a handsome man who is never home and a full closet, but an empty place in your heart where his love should be.

Making Him Wait Won't Make Him A Better Man

"If he's the wrong man, having a rule that says you won't have sex with him before 'X' amount of days won't change him. At the end of the waiting period, he'll still be the same wrong man."

When he's wrong, he's wrong; time won't magically make him right. All you will be doing is postponing your inevitable disappointment and heartbreak. Now, I'm not saying that you should rush into it either. What I am saying is there is no set amount of time that will allow you to determine that man's worth, it will vary. However, the more time you give it, the more time you will have to evaluate whether or not he's someone you want to go to the next level with.

My thoughts: be patient and go with your gut. You will know better based on how you feel rather than by what date it is. Just know, there are no guarantees and in the end, time won't change who he is.

A Man That Just Takes

"In a relationship, you can never give enough to a man who is willing to take everything from you."

Some men are just takers. They don't understand that a relationship is about giving and taking...it's about balance. To these men, it's always about them. Being able to compromise, in the name of moving the relationship forward, is a concept they cannot grasp.

It's this type of man who, after you've done everything for him, still comes to the door of the relationship with his hand out expecting more. Then, he has the audacity to try to make you feel bad when you finally say, "enough!"

When He Wants To Change Who You Are

"Any man who makes you feel as if you have to change who you are, as a person, to be with him, is a man that will leave you as soon as he meets the woman he's trying to make you out to be."

For the most part, most men have an idea of what they want in a woman from the beginning. In his mind, he already has a picture of what she should look like and what qualities he would like her to possess. With that in mind, if he's trying to change you, what are the chances of him leaving you if he ever meets someone that fits that picture in his head?

Just something for you to think about before you put yourself in that type of situation.

In my opinion, if he truly loves you, he will love you for the person you are, not the person he wants you to be.

Questionable Intentions

"You need a man to be upfront and honest with you, from the beginning, about his intentions. The right man will be; however, the wrong man will let months, or even years go by before he finally gets up the courage to tell you that he's not ready to commit."

Most men know, even before they approach you, what their initial intentions are. His plans may change as the relationship progresses, but regardless, he usually has an idea as to what his initial intentions are from the beginning.

When a man strings you along and leaves you in the dark, it could mean a few different things. One, he's not sure if he wants the same things you want out of the relationship. This causes him to be afraid to tell you he's not ready to commit, out of fear you may break the relationship off. Or two, he knows exactly what he wants from the relationship (i.e. sex, money, etc.) and he knows you wouldn't waste your time with him if you knew his real intentions.

Either way, if he doesn't have the courage to be honest with you, that lack of honesty will eventually leave you disappointed and, in some cases, brokenhearted.

His Insecurities

"The only time a man feels the need to tear you down is when he's feeling insecure. Because of his insecurities and low self-esteem, he then tries to make you feel smaller in order to make himself feel bigger."

A man with insecurities is a very difficult man to deal with, especially for a strong, ambitious woman. Anything you do to improve yourself, he will more than likely view it as a threat to his manhood. He is the type of man who will support you, but only to an extent. Meaning, he will support you as long as what you are doing doesn't threaten his status in any way. If it does, you will begin to notice his support turn into discouragement. The positive reinforcement, which you once received, will slowly turn into negativity. This will often start with subtle comments and remarks and escalate to outright anger and aggression towards you. That is his way of trying to compensate for his own insecurities.

You see, if you begin to do well for yourself, he sees himself as losing that power over you. In his mind, you may start to think that you don't need him and one day you might decide that you don't have to put up with his nonsense anymore and leave. In order to ensure that doesn't happen, he feels he has to keep you mentally feeling as if you're nothing without him, thus reducing the chances of you ever leaving and increasing your perceived dependency on him.

Abusive Men

"There are a lot of things in this world that you, as a woman, could be afraid of, but your man should not be one of them."

A man that loves you will always assume the role of your protector, not your aggressor. Abusive men, however, are like cancer to you. You have to identify their type early on and cut them out of your life. Whether it's mental, physical, or emotional abuse, please understand that his only purpose is to eat away at you until there's nothing left.

Find a way out as soon as possible. The longer he stays in your life, the greater the risk that you might not survive the battle…literally.

He Feels

Entitled

"Some men feel a sense of entitlement...like you owe them something, when in reality, you don't owe him anything! He owes it to himself to get his stuff together. You can support him...you can even help him but ultimately, it's his responsibility, not yours."

Here's my public service announcement for the day: Ladies, stop carrying these grown men! It's okay to support him and even to help him to an extent; that's part of being in a relationship. However, this is true only up until a certain point. After that, he has to get up on his own two feet and do what men do. If you carry him for too long, you're no longer helping him...you're hurting him.

Emotionally Lazy Men

"Whatever you do, never chase a man. Why?
Because it'll make him emotionally lazy
and he will feel like he doesn't have to do
anything to meet your emotional needs."

Think about it; if you're doing everything from the beginning, what is his incentive to do anything after you two get together? In the end, you'll find yourself assuming the proactive role throughout the relationship because that's what he'll be used to. He will have no reason to change because you'll have already shown him that he can do absolutely nothing and you will still be willing to do everything.

When He Complains About Doing Things That Make You Happy

"The wrong man will do something nice for you and complain the whole time while doing it. He'll then expect you to be happy, not realizing that his attitude ruined everything."

Let's say you love to walk along the beach, but every time he takes you, he complains. He thinks he is earning brownie points by taking you when, in fact, he's losing points. Sooner or later, you'll stop asking him to go with you. He may think he's finally convinced you that walking along the beach is boring but he hasn't. You still love walking along the beach… you still want to walk along the beach…you just are no longer interested in doing it with him.

The right man, however, will do it because he wants to make you happy. He won't ruin your moment with his petty personal complaints. After all, he is making you happy and at the end of the day, in his mind, that's what it's all about.

You Could Be Doing Everything Right

"You could be doing everything right: working, cooking, cleaning, great sex...everything. But if it's for the wrong man, that still won't be enough to keep him."

Remember this: a good man can't be kept and the wrong man isn't worth keeping. So then you may ask, "What does a woman have to do to keep a man?" The answer is this...let go of the idea that it is within your power to keep him and focus more on finding a good man that loves and respects you enough to want to stay; therein lies the secret.

You see, you could be doing all the right things, but

if that man doesn't love, respect, and appreciate you and the things you do, it will all be for nothing.

NOTES:

List the main qualities of the wrong man that are absolute deal breakers to you.

_____

_____

_____

_____

_____

Now list how, in the past, you've missed these qualities or reasons why you've tolerated them.

_____

_____

_____

_____

_____

_____

Finally, write down how, in the future, you will better guard yourself against these qualities.

_____

_____

_____

_____

_____

CHAPTER

A WEAK MAN

"A weak man is intimidated by a strong woman. Not because of what he thinks she can do to him physically, but rather because of what he knows she won't allow him to do to her mentally and emotionally."

Broken

"Any man who tries to break you mentally, is already broken both mentally and emotionally."

A secure man understands that the strength of the relationship is found in the union and not the individual. A strong man and a strong woman create a strong union. If one or the other is weak, the relationship suffers.

In other words, it defeats the purpose for you to try to build a relationship with a broken man whose intent is only to tear you down.

Weak Men Are Incapable Of Sweeping You Off Your Feet

"A weak man is incapable of sweeping you off your feet. Why? Because he doesn't have the emotional strength to lift your spirit."

When I speak of a man's true strength, I'm not speaking of his physical strength, I'm talking about his mental, emotional, and spiritual strength. That's where a man's true power lies. Any man can pick you up physically, but it takes an exceptional man to lift you up emotionally and spiritually; that is something a weak man cannot do.

CHAPTER

Four

SECRECY
VS.
PRIVACY

His Right
To
Privacy

"Just because he has a right to his privacy in the
relationship, doesn't mean he has a right to keep secrets
from you."

So the big question is how do you find out if he's
keeping any secrets if you don't invade his privacy?
The answer is...you can't. You are going to have to
cross the line for confirmation and personally, I don't see
anything wrong with you confirming the loyalty and the
trustworthiness of the one you entrust with your heart.
We confirm everything else: hotel reservations, dinner
reservations, payments, etc.... If there is nothing there,
all the better. Confirmation simply proves or disproves

your beliefs, one way or the other. I have found that the ones who rely heavily on the "privacy" position, are often the ones with the most to hide.

Having said that, I also know that some of you won't cross that line because it opens you up to the same and you're not willing to take that risk. Why? Because some of you have your own secrets to keep.

His Secrets

"If he decides to keep one little secret from you, it will have the power to ruin your whole relationship. Not necessarily because of the secret in and of itself, but because of the thousand lies that he'll have to tell you to keep it."

Why Is He So Defensive

"A man who can't answer your questions, when you ask, without getting defensive, is often a man who is keeping more than just the answer from you."

Have you ever asked a question where his response was so defensive, you began to think that something just wasn't right...like he was keeping something from you? If you have, you were probably right.

When a man gets defensive, that's usually his guilty conscience shining through. Your female intuition will sense it; that's what it's designed for.

My thoughts...you need to get to the bottom of it immediately. Don't let your mind override your gut or you'll possibly find yourself investing months or even years more into someone just to find out, in the end, it was all a waste of time.

You Have A Right To Know

"Just because you ask a question, doesn't necessarily mean you don't trust him; some things, just by being in the relationship, you have a right to know."

There is absolutely nothing wrong with you asking a question. Any man that would get upset with you for simply asking a question, probably has something to hide. Think about it. If you're asking a question to get clarification on an issue and the answer could possibly prevent a misunderstanding or an argument, what would be a good reason not to answer the question? The only reason I can think of is that he has something to hide.

What You Don't Know

*They say, "What you don't know can't hurt you," but I
disagree. What you don't know can and will hurt you.
And the longer it takes for you to find out, the more it
will hurt you in the end.*

I f you feel there's something going on, get to the bottom of it quickly. Don't be afraid to ask the question. If you try to fool yourself into thinking you can block the doubt out, it will eventually begin to eat you up inside. Then your happiness will turn to sorrow and your love for him into frustration and resentment. It's not always the question that eats you up but more so the idea of not having the answer to the question that wears on you.

NOTES:

_____

_____

_____

_____

_____

_____

_____

_____

_____

CHAPTER

TRUST

"When the trust is gone, everything else will soon follow."

Make Him Earn It

"Just because he earned your trust today, doesn't mean he is incapable of violating your trust tomorrow."

Trust is not a one-time thing; it's a constant work in progress. Every day you should be consistently re-evaluating to see if he deserves your trust. That doesn't necessarily mean you don't trust him, it simply means you're not naive to human nature.

Think about it; every man who has ever cheated on you, at some point, you considered him to be trustworthy.

Emotionally Drained

*"When you don't trust the person you're with, it
becomes physically and emotionally exhausting for you
to stay in the relationship."*

Trust just makes everything work smoother. When trust is absent, you end up spending more time mad, not necessarily at what he is doing, but more so at what you think he might be doing. This, as time goes on, will cause you to feel frustrated and exhausted.

CHAPTER

UNFAITHFUL

*"If he loves and respects you, he won't cheat. If he does
cheat, one or both of the above is missing."*

Its Not An Accident

"Cheating is never an accident;
it is a conscious decision."

The unfaithful often refuse to accept personal responsibility for their actions and instead, they resort to trying to make you feel as if somehow your actions or inactions are to blame. Don't buy into it! It is never your fault. It was their choice to cheat; therefore, they shoulder 100% of the blame. If there was something you were or were not doing that was causing so much of an issue, they should have come to you first. If the issue couldn't be resolved, they had one of the following two choices to make: leave then or stay and try to work it out. Either way, cheating on you should not have been one of those options.

His Apology

"*When he apologizes, just know that he is not sorry
that he cheated...he's sorry you found out.*"

In some cases, he may feel as if an apology should suffice; however, an apology, at this point, is like throwing salt on an open wound. Why? Because apologies are for accidents or for when someone does something and, at the time, they had no idea it would hurt you.

Cheating, on the other hand, is a conscious decision, thus ruling out the idea that it was an "accident." Plus, at the time he cheated, he knew that his actions would hurt you; thereby ruling out the argument that he "didn't know."

So, you may ask, why is he actually apologizing? I'll tell you. It's not because he cheated and it's not because he hurt you. He is sorry that you found out; that's the one thing he didn't plan for.

You Believe The Lies

You believe the lies because you're afraid of the truth.
So when he feeds you the lines
about where he's been all night,
you've preconditioned yourself to believe the lies
to be true.
While deep down inside you fight with yourself,
going back and forth as you pray for help.
So maybe my inspiration for this book was divine
or maybe it was something I picked up in your
Comments while reading between the lines.
We all have our suspicions but my advice to you,
is you should listen to your conscience...
that's God's way of talking directly to you.

The Feeling Of Betrayal

"When a man cheats on a woman, it's not so much the physical act that hurts her; it's the feeling of her being emotionally betrayed by the one person she loved and trusted to never to do such a thing...that's what hurts the most."

NOTES:

List the top 3 signs from the past, that you ignored, which warned you that he was cheating and promise yourself that you will never ignore these signs again.

_____

_____

_____

CHAPTER

SECOND
CHANCES

"Some people get a second chance while others don't because some people are willing to change while others won't."

Just Because
You
Miss Him

*"Just because you miss him, doesn't mean you should
take him back."*

It's okay to miss him; that's normal. Every relationship has its good moments and those moments often create great memories. Just remember, you left for a reason. And at the time you left, that reason outweighed those memories. Now, I'm not saying you should never give someone a second chance. There are times when people change and it's up to you as to whether or not you believe their change is enough for you to take them back. However, don't let loneliness, or the fact that you miss them, cloud your judgment to the point where you find yourself back in the same bad relationship you just got out of.

Forgiveness Doesn't Always Equal A Second Chance

❦

"Just because you are willing to forgive him, doesn't necessarily mean he gets an automatic second chance."

Your willingness to forgive him shows that you are strong enough to be able to move forward without holding it against him. That doesn't necessarily mean you are willing to put yourself back in the same situation for him to hurt you again.

Your decision to give him a second chance should be largely based on whether or not you believe whatever has happened will happen again. If you think it won't, then ask yourself if that alone is a good enough reason to go back into the relationship. If you believe it will occur again, walk away now before you have to run away later.

NOTES:

List all of the reasons why you believe you should give him a second chance.

_____

_____

_____

_____

_____

_____

_____

List all of the reasons why you believe you should not give him a second chance.

_____

_____

_____

_____

_____

_____

_____

_____

_____

Now compare both lists and make your decision based on what's best for you.

CHAPTER

YOU CAN'T
CHANGE HIM

*"He'll only change if he wants to change; my question is,
if you don't like the man he is today,
why are you with him now?"*

The Reason He Changes

*"You can't change a man, but you can definitely be a
big part of the reason he decides to change."*

For some men, all they need is a reason to change; the right woman, at the right time, in the right man's life, could very well be that reason. But be careful, the wrong man will not be able to recognize you as a good woman and he will take your time and waste it. He'll act like he's changed for just long enough to get what he wants from you. After he's accomplished his goal, he will revert back to his old ways leaving you physically, emotionally and, in some cases, financially drained.

Some of you have dealt with this man in the past, while others are still dealing with him now. You may even begin to doubt yourself and think there's something wrong with you. Rest your mind; it's not that you aren't the right woman, it's just that he is the wrong man.

The Real Problem

"Sometimes, him being the wrong man isn't the real problem. The real problem is you deciding to give him a chance, knowing he's the wrong man, thinking you can change him."

Never go into a relationship thinking you can change a man that has already shown you his true intentions are not what you want.

In the end, he won't change and you'll end up frustrated, heartbroken, and alone wishing you had done things differently.

CHAPTER

Nine

WASTED TIME

"It's impossible to hold onto a relationship when the other person has already decided to let it go."

Single And Alone

*"A strong woman would rather be single and alone
than to waste her time being in a relationship and
sleeping with a man who makes her feel like
she doesn't even exist."*

S ometimes, you're left with only two choices: (1) Sleep alone and be physically cold or (2) waste your time sleeping next to someone who cares nothing about you and wake up in the morning feeling cold emotionally.

When He Loses Your Respect

❧

*"One of the hardest things you'll ever try to do is
continue to love someone you no longer respect."*

Respect and trust are at the very foundation of any healthy relationship. Without them, everything else quickly disappears; everything except love. Love doesn't disappear right away. It first slowly turns into frustration, followed by resentment. This evolution will leave you, not with the memories of the love you once shared, but with the feelings of resentment and regret that you now feel.

Frustrated

❧

"One of the most frustrating positions you, as a good woman, could ever find yourself in, is in a relationship with a man who makes you feel like you're still single."

Being in a relationship with a man that has no time for you, shows you no affection, and makes you feel like, half the time, you're still single... what's the point?

I can think of a lot of good reasons why you would want to be in a relationship but being lonely isn't one of them.

My thoughts...talk to him. Don't try to ignore the feeling because it will only get worse. Explain to him how you feel and give him the opportunity to make the necessary adjustments. If he makes those adjustments, great. If he doesn't, then the balls back in your court. You can either accept it or reject it, but the choice is yours.

When He Doesn't Love You And You Know It

"Some of you will fall asleep tonight and dream of what it would be like to be truly loved, then wake up in the morning and choose to waste your time on a man you know doesn't love you."

You can't complain about being in a situation that you have the power to change but choose not to. If you know it's not going anywhere, don't waste your time.

*"True love is an exciting experience...one that should
never cause you to feel emotionally lonely."*

ven when there is a physical distance between
you, the emotional connection should still be
there. You should be able to close your eyes, on
the darkest nights, and still feel their presence...to be
physically alone, yet spiritually accompanied by their
very essence. If ever there comes a time when you feel
emotionally lonely in a relationship, it may be because
what was...no longer is.

In Love With The Idea

*Some of you are more "in love" with the idea of "being
in love" than you are "in love" with the
person you are with.*

So you've created a fantasy world in your head and
in this world, you've made your relationship out to
be more than what it really is. Because you're in
love with the "idea of being in love" and you want it so
bad, you ignore all the signs that tell you this person is
wrong for you. You are so ready to believe that he is who
you want him to be that, even when he shows you that
he is not you ignore it.

Your friends, the ones you trust the most, have tried
to warn you, but you've blown them off by saying, "They
don't know" or "they don't understand" or "they're just

hating on you because you're happy." My question is, "happy with what?" Are you happy with the idea or the reality?

Remember this: all fantasies come to an end. At some point, you'll have to deal with the reality of the matter and the fact that he isn't really what you want or need. Then you're left disappointed and stuck with two choices: settle or move on after wasting all your time on something that never was.

Why Are You Still Here?

"If you don't love me, why are you still here?
You standing there only makes it worse.
Please, just walk away.
I promise, I won't hate you if you do
but I will if you don't."

They say, If you want to understand how someone else feels, you have to be able to put yourself in their shoes. So, I asked myself, "If I were you and someone strung me along, how would I feel?" That was the first thing that came to mind.

What Hurts The Most

"What hurts you the most is not the fact that it's over, but rather that you chose to waste your time with him in the first place."

NOTES:

_____

_____

_____

CHAPTER

HEARTBREAK

"Have you ever felt like your heart had been ripped right out of your chest... like when they walked out the door, they took with them your very last breath?"

He Can't Love You

"One of the most disappointing things that you, as a woman, could ever go through is to fall in love with a man that can't love and respect you because he hasn't learned to love and respect himself yet."

Emotionally Stuck

"The worst feeling you can have is the feeling of being stuck in a physical relationship with someone you have already emotionally separated from."

The True Frustration Of Heartbreak

"A woman's tears don't necessarily come from one heartbreak, but rather they come from the accumulation of years of heartbreak and the frustration that you feel after putting everything you have into your relationships, day after day, month after month, and year after year, and still ending up with the same heartbreaking results."

"A woman's teardrops are the unspoken words
of her soul.
They write the story of her pain with disappearing ink
and with every stroke,
I try to understand before I wipe away the words
from her face,
In hopes that, as the tears dry, true love will be the
reason all her pain has been erased."

When The Love Is Real

*"When your love is real, it's hard to just stop
loving someone...even after they've proven to you over
and over again that they don't deserve your love."*

That's what makes breaking up so hard to do. You know it's time to go, but love just won't let you walk away. Real love wants you to give them another chance, to try just one more time to make it work, even when deep down inside you know...he'll never change.

Your Broken Heart

*Does a woman's broken heart ever truly heal
or do you simply become stronger and find better ways
to conceal the pain?
You see, I might not know your name, but you can't fool
me with the lines,
telling me you don't care about him anymore, but I can
see it in your eyes that he hurt you.
Don't be ashamed of the pain: embrace it.
Don't turn your back on the pain: face it.
Let it all out and release it to the wind
and when you've gotten it all out, there will be just
enough room in your heart for you to finally love again.*

Only a new love can help repair the damage left by an old one. Whether it be the love from another, a spiritual love, the love of self or all of the above, only love has that power.

It's Okay

It's okay.
It's okay for you to miss him.
It's okay for you to feel angry.
It's okay for you to feel sad and even to cry...
It's okay.
It's okay for you to wonder whether or not you made
the right decision...
It's okay.

B reaking up can be quite the emotional roller coaster ride. Just know, when the ride is over and you've gotten it all out of your system...it's okay to move on.

NOTES:

Sometimes it helps to write it all out...

_____

_____

_____

_____

_____

_____

_____

_____

_____

CHAPTER

Eleven

THE COURAGE TO MOVE ON

"A strong woman won't give up on the relationship until she is completely fed up and her leaving is the only option she has left.
And even then...it's hard for her to do."

She's Tired

"When a strong woman finally gives up, it's not because she's weak or because she no longer loves her man. To put it in the simplest terms...she's just tired. She's tired of the games...she's tired of the sleepless nights...she's tired of feeling like she's all alone and the only one trying... she's tired."

Some might say that a woman is weak for giving up on a relationship, but I disagree. When you've done all you can and you've reached that point where you feel physically, emotionally, and spiritually drained, your only option left is to leave. Not because you want to but because you have to...for your own sanity and peace of mind.

A Strong Woman's Cry

"Who can hear the cries of a strong woman who cries only on the inside while the world compliments her on how strong she is and on the beautiful smile that they see on the outside."

Who can you run to when you are the one that everyone runs to? Who can you call when you are the one that everyone calls? When it just seems like the pressure is getting to be too much and you feel like you can't hold it together much longer, who do you, the strong woman that everyone else looks to for strength, who do you turn to?

Sometimes, the only right answer is a spiritual one.

Being Strong Is Not An Option

"A strong woman knows that being strong is not an option for her, it's a necessity."

So, every day she wakes up and meets the world and all of its challenges head on. But sometimes, at the end of the day, when all is said and done and she finally closes the door, she cries. Not because she's weak, but because it's hard being strong, day after day, knowing that if you don't do it, no one will.

The soft cries that most will never hear slowly disappear as the new day comes and you rise once again to be the strong, confident woman you are.

You Still Remember

You still remember, but you will never forget.
You still remember how he used to make you smile, but
you will never forget how he used to always
talk down to you.
You still remember how you first met, but the day he
called you out your name, that's a day
you will never forget.
You see, it's hard for a strong woman to hold on to a
man that has disrespected her. And though he
apologized and you accepted,
you didn't do it for his sake, but for your own
peace of mind.
So as you walked out that door, leaving that man be-
hind, you sighed. Because although you forgave him
you knew you could never forget, and that's why to this
day, you've never looked back.

The Strength To Let Go

*"The reality is that sometimes, it takes more strength to
let go than it does to keep holding on."*

When a woman stands with her back to the
wind and her face to the sun, raises her
head, exhales and finally lets go, that's a
powerful moment for her. So many feelings run through
her body at that time. She feels happy, yet saddened;
excited, yet afraid about the chapter to come. But one
thing she knows for sure is that she is finally free to find
her own happiness.

The Power To Endure

*Late at night I toss and I turn as if in a storm
on the open sea.
I see the lightning in your eyes and hear the thunder in
your voice and I know that you call for me.
As our souls awaken with the anticipation of
embracing the moment before it's gone.
For I know you have walked for thousands of miles
and you have struggled for so long.
Though your struggles have been hard,
your battle scars they testify
to all the pain you have endured, which can be viewed
through unopened eyes.
Yet you ask not for sympathy, not even when
your days are long.
For in you is the power to endure and the
strength to carry on.*

So Blessed Is The Smile

So blessed is the smile of the woman, who for years has known the pain of being cheated on, the agony of being under appreciated, disrespected and belittled by a man she once loved and trusted.

So blessed is the smile of the woman, who for years put her heart and soul into a relationship and got nothing in return.

So blessed is the smile of the woman that has been forged by the fire and the many years of the lessons learned.

So blessed is the smile of the woman, who one day stood up and said, "Enough is enough! I deserve better than this! I deserve to be with someone who loves, respects, and adores me! I deserve my own happiness!"

You see, it's been some time now since she got up the courage to walk out and it hasn't been easy.

She spent some nights crying herself to sleep and other

*nights second guessing herself on whether or not
she had done the right thing, but she never went back.
So I say,
"So blessed is the smile of the strong woman because after all you've
been through, you've finally found your own happiness
and that smile represents the new you."*

Lessons Learned

*"The ones that are the hardest to get over are often the
ones that teach you the greatest lesson."*

For the ones you have loved, they've shown you the infinite possibilities of happiness. As for the ones you have lost, they've reminded you of the tremendous pains of heartbreak. To all of them, you say, "Thank you." It's because of them that you now stand there the beautiful, strong, and independent woman that you are.

Forgive For Your Sake

❧

"When you forgive, you don't do it for the other person's sake, you do it for your own sanity and peace of mind."

In the end, when you hold onto your anger, you're hurting no one but yourself. Meanwhile, they go about living their lives as they wish while your anger and resentment allow them to continue to ruin yours. You, in essence, have become the surrogate to all the pain, frustration, and heartache that they once caused you. Now, they don't need to do anything but sit back, enjoy their life, and watch you be miserable.

It doesn't have to be that way; you can take that power away from them simply by forgiving them and letting it go. I'm not saying you have to forget, don't forget. Forgetting what they've done would erase the memory and in the memory is where you find the lesson. However, forgiving removes the weight of the past from your shoulders and allows you to move forward without them.

The past is what it is; you can't change it. What you can do is learn from it and use that to make better decisions in the future. Will it be easy…no. Will you have your moments…yes, but over time, you'll find peace in knowing they no longer have that power over you. Now, when you see them you can finally smile and say to yourself, "I'm finally free from you."

Never Feel Trapped

❧

You should never feel trapped in a relationship;
you always have options. He may want you to feel as if
you don't and that he is the only option available to you
but he's not. The decision as to whether or not you stay
or leave is yours to make and yours only. It may not be
an easy choice, but it is still your choice to make; you
have that power. You have the power to free yourself
of the negativity and to find happiness. You have the
power to live your life the way you choose,
rather than as someone else dictates.
You have the power…use it.

CHAPTER

TIME
FOR YOU

"If you can't see the beauty of your life from where you are now, remove the obstacles in front of you and look again."

Help Yourself

"Sometimes, the only person who can help you is you."

Your friends can support you, they can cheer you on and be there for you, but in the end, you have to be the one to make the hard decisions and make the changes. No one can do that for you but you.

Do What Makes You Happy

❧

"Ladies...for just one moment, stop worrying about what everyone else thinks and do what makes you happy."

I realize that most of your time is spent tending to the wants and needs of your children, your career, and everyone else. You are constantly running, from before the sun rises until well after it sets, trying to hold all of the pieces to your life's puzzle together. Ironically, somewhere through it all, you lose track of the most important piece...you. Then, when you try to take time for yourself, you get "grief for it" and in some instances, you even get accused of being "selfish." Interestingly enough, the ones that say you are being "selfish" are usually the ones you give all of your attention to. So, your question to them should be, "Am I really being selfish or are you?"

Never feel guilty for wanting to take time for yourself. After all you do for everyone else…you've earned it. Take time for you.

Fall In Love With You Again

Sometimes…you simply have to make time for you. Find the time to take yourself out on a date so that you can reacquaint yourself with who you are and what you want out of life. If you do this often enough, you never know, you might just find yourself falling in love with "you" all over again.

NOTES:

Keep track of all the things you do, that are just for you, and describe how they make you feel about yourself.

_____

_____

_____

_____

_____

_____

_____

_____

CHAPTER

Thirteen

THE FEAR OF STARTING OVER

"There's nothing wrong with holding on and there's nothing wrong with letting go. The trick is deciding which one is best for you."

She's Not Afraid
To Love

"She's had her heart broken, yet she's not afraid to love;
what she is afraid of is wasting any more years
of her life loving and supporting a man just to,
in the end, have her heart broken and find herself
having to start all over again."

The Fear Of Being Vulnerable

❧❧❧

"The feeling of being vulnerable is one of the scariest things about falling in love. But the idea of putting it all out there and loving without pause or regret...that's what makes it exciting."

With great risk comes either great sorrow or great reward. I say, trust your judgment and take a chance! If you're wrong, the pain will be only temporary. However, if you're right, you could find enough happiness to last you a lifetime.

Holding On To The Past

"As long as you hold on to your anger for the wrong man of the past, he will forever have control over your ability to be happy in the future."

A lot of you have moved on physically, but you still carry the pain and the anger that he caused you inside.

Give yourself a fair chance to find true happiness. Now is the time to finally let him go.

The Man Of Your Dreams

"Let go of your fears of starting over"

As a young girl, you dreamed of the man he would be. Some of you have found that man and others have settled. Those of you who have settled, late at night, still wonder what life would be like if you had not settled. Your dreams of happiness run down your cheeks and turn into tears of sorrow as you cry yourself to sleep.

Remember, in life you have choices; let go of your fear of starting over and do what's best for you. It's never too late to be happy...the choice is yours.

CHAPTER

BEAUTIFUL STRONG WOMAN

You just have to say to yourself, "I'm not willing to accept anything less than what I deserve! I am smart! I am beautiful! I am a good woman, and I deserve to be happy!" It all starts with you.

Take Control
Today

Today, take control of your life
and be the beautiful, strong woman you dreamed,
as a little girl,
you would someday grow up to be.
Some of you may have already forgotten that dream
and others may have settled.
Today, I am here to remind you of it.
Stop living someone else's dream and start living your
own. Remember, that little girl inside still
believes in you...don't let her down.

Be You

"Be the woman you want to be, not the woman everyone else expects you to be."

God makes no mistakes. If you look at it from that perspective, you will see that you are a perfect creation of what he intended when he created you. Be proud of who you are. After all, you're not only a one in a million...you're a once in a lifetime.

You Are Beautiful

"You are beautiful just the way you are."

We all have those days when, for whatever reason, we just don't feel that beautiful and a reminder would be nice. If today is your day, let me remind you...you are beautiful just the way you are.

"More often than not, it's the little things that
matter most."

I hope he noticed that you had your hair done in a different style or the fact that you painted your nails that new color you've been wanting to try. I hope he noticed that new outfit you bought to wear just for him. I hope he noticed and complimented you on them. If not, let me be the first...you look amazing!

The Perfect You

"I hope when you woke up this morning, you looked in the mirror and saw exactly what I see when I look at you... an incredibly beautiful woman who is unique and deserving of all the love and attention that a good man has to offer."

A Strong Woman's Smile

"A strong woman with a beautiful smile is attractive, but a strong woman with a beautiful mind is addictive."

In The Lake There Lies A Reflection

*In the lake there lies a reflection, a mere perfected
image of you.
If you sit quietly by her bedside, she'll move closer
and closer to you.
If you smile, she'll smile back. Whenever you touch
her, she'll react.
In the lake there lies a reflection, if you love her, she will
always love you back.*

J ust a reminder, no matter what you are going
through, love yourself first and you will always be
loved; no one can take that away from you.

A Strong Woman's Walls Around Her Heart

I love a woman who has built up strong walls around her heart. It tells me that you've been through some things and, not only are you a survivor, but from those experiences, you've learned how to better protect yourself. You've also learned the true value of your love and now getting close to your heart is not that easy. If a man wants your love, he's going to have to prove himself worthy before you give him the honor of replacing that wall and assuming the role of your heart's protector.

In my opinion, there are mainly three types of people who would criticize you for having a strong wall around your heart: Those that are too lazy to work for your love, those that have never been through the lesson, and those that have been through it but still haven't learned.

A Strong Woman Is Self-Defined

A strong woman is self-defined. She knows that the only definition of her that matters is her own.

You define yourself. You have total control over who you are as a woman; no man has the power to take that from you unless you give it to him.

To My Beautiful Strong Woman

You know you are beautiful, not because he tells you, but because ever since you were a young girl, you have always known that you would someday grow up to be a beautiful, strong woman. You're not arrogant or conceited; you're humble, yet confident. There's a certain strength about you that cannot be ignored.

Strong, confident men find your strength to be incredibly attractive while weaker, less confident men find it to be intimidating and feel threatened by it. Your strength is both your greatest blessing and your greatest curse. Your greatest curse because many men have fallen

short causing you to spend countless nights alone
wondering if you were asking too much but you're not.
In fact, it is your strength which allows you to maintain your high
standards, through all those lonely nights, because you know that
one day, the right man will reveal himself to you. Then and only
then, will you lower your walls and allow yourself to become
vulnerable to fall hopelessly in love without fear or pause.

To my Beautiful, Strong Woman: Be strong... Be patient. The right man is out there searching relentlessly, through all the nonsense, looking for you. Give him time.

CHAPTER

SETTING A NEW STANDARD

"The quality of the man you choose will only be as good as the standards by which you use to choose him."

*Never Lower
Your Standards*

❧

*"Don't ever think that you will avoid being
disappointed by lowering your standards for a man.
In the end, not only will you still be disappointed by
him, but you will also be disappointed in yourself for
ever having lowered your standards in the first place."*

Be selective. Every man should not meet your
standards. There's nothing wrong with you deciding not to waste your time on a man that
you've determined is a waste of time.

Having standards doesn't mean you're "stuck-up"
or "conceited," it means you're a strong woman, who
knows what she wants and is not willing to settle for any-

thing less. There is nothing wrong with that. In fact, as a man…I respect that.

Never feel bad for having high standards; it's part of your process for weeding out the wrong man.

Be The "Only" One

Why settle for being a "side" or a "main" when there is a good man out there waiting to make you his "only."

D on't make yourself unavailable for the right man because you became impatient and settled for the wrong man.

Think about it for a minute; if he doesn't value you enough to commit to making you his "only," he most certainly is not emotionally wealthy enough to be able to afford your love.

You Are Extraordinary

❧

"When you are extraordinary, ordinary just won't do."

You are an extraordinary woman who is capable of accomplishing anything and everything you set your heart and mind to. You should settle for nothing less than a man who, not only recognizes this, but also encourages you at every opportunity to be the absolute best you can be. He should also be a man who is secure enough in himself and the relationship to be able to take a step back and be your biggest fan when it finally comes time for you to shine and do your thing.

Friends With Benefits

*"Friends with benefits" is a creative way of him
saying he thinks you're good enough to sleep with, but
not worthy of his loyalty and commitment.*

No matter how you look at it, for you as a good woman, there are no long-term benefits to this type of relationship. I don't care how "Acceptable" Hollywood tries to make it seem. In the end, what do you have: no commitment, no loyalty, no love...nothing. All the things that really matter to you, as a good woman, you don't get. All you have is the instant physical gratification and when that's gone, you're left with nothing. You deserve better.

Strong, Single And Happy

"She's single, not because she can't find a man, but because she's waiting for the right man to come along and make her feel so secure in the relationship that loving him just comes natural and easy."

Don't ever let anyone make you feel like being single is a bad thing. Take your time, be patient, and wait for the right one.

It's almost like buying fruit at the grocery store. You don't just walk up, grab the first piece of fruit you see and put it in your basket. No! You pick it up, squeeze it, look it over and if it's not what you want, you put it back. Besides, everyone knows that the best fruit is on the bottom. You have to dig a little to get to the highest quality fruit.

Well, men are kind of the same. You have to take your time, check them out and if you don't like him, put him back! Why? Because at the end of the day, if you rush and take the wrong one home, you're the one that has to deal with him!

Be Patient

***

"Somewhere out there, there's a good man just as frustrated as you are that he has not found you yet; be patient. He won't give up on you...don't you dare give up on him."

If you've ever been somewhere and were lost and needed someone to come find you, you'd know that one of the first things they tell you is "stay right there. I'm on my way." The reason they say that is because if you keep moving, it makes it more difficult for them to find you. Well, the same applies here. You have to stop moving around and wasting all your time on men that you know can't or won't meet your emotional needs and sit still and be patient long enough to be found by the right man who can and will.

Too Many To Settle

"There are too many men out there for you to settle on one that doesn't make you happy. If he's not acting right, let him know. If he's not willing to fix it, let him go."

Even a good man can have issues, but as long as he's willing to work through them with you, to move the relationship forward, there's still the possibility of things working out.

On the other hand, if he's not willing to work with you to fix the problem, then sometimes, you even have to let the good ones go.

The Same Applies To You

"In your relationship, never settle for less than what you deserve. At the same time, never think you deserve more out of a relationship than you are willing to put into it."

Be realistic in your expectations. When I say you should never settle, that doesn't absolve you of your responsibility to meet the same expectations that you set for them. If your expectations are high, then your own level of performance and commitment should be equally as high. You should expect to get out of it what you put into it. Nothing more, nothing less.

The Ticking Clock

*Don't ever let the "ticking of the clock" force you into
settling for a man you know isn't right for you. In the
end, is it not better to be single and happy for 5 years,
than to wake up one morning and realize you have
wasted the last 5 years of your life with someone you
knew would never make you happy in the first place?*

This is just a different way of looking at things.
Whatever you do, makes sure it's right for you:
not your friends, not family, not anyone else...
do what's best for you.

Time To Choose

"The more time you take, in the beginning, to choose the right man, the less time you'll waste, in the end, dealing with the wrong one."

You have worked too hard and come too far, to get where you are today, to let a man with no vision or no direction slow you down. Take your time.

STAY FOCUSED!

Your New List

Use the following page to write down your new standards. Don't focus on financial or physical attributes, those are things you want. I want you to concentrate on writing down what you need emotionally, as a woman, from a man.

In short, I'm asking you to describe, on one page, what the right man is to you. When you finish, review what you've written and commit it to memory. As you grow, adjust it accordingly.

Now, I want you to promise yourself, no matter how long your days are or how lonely your nights may be, you will never settle for anything less than what's on that one page of paper.

NOTES:

CHAPTER

Sixteen

SOME THINGS
FOR YOU
TO
THINK ABOUT

Important Impression

"The most important impression a man can make on you is not the first impression, but rather a lasting impression that only comes from consistency over time."

Even the wrong man can play the role of the right man in the beginning. Don't be so impressed by his first impression. The first impression is the easy part. It's the lasting impression that takes all the work.

Don't Confuse Comfort For Love

Don't confuse being "comfortable" for being "in love."

Some of you are in a relationship because you are "in love" and some of you are in a relationship simply because you are "comfortable" in it and afraid of change.

Remember, just because you are comfortable, doesn't mean you're in love. How to tell the difference? Ask yourself this question, "Why am I here?" If you have no answer or you have to justify your answer through logic and not emotion, then that's comfort. If you're there because of love, you'll know because your answer will be an emotional one and just thinking about the answer will cause you to smile.

Some Men Would Say Anything

Some men would say "anything" to get what they want,
but you have to be willing to believe "anything"
to give it to them.

It's less about what he says and more about what you choose to believe. Be more selective and patient. Knowing that most men will say anything means that you can't believe everything. Remember, without consistent actions, over time, his words have no value.

Potential Means Nothing

❦

"You being able to see the potential in a man means nothing until he sees it in himself."

You can see all the potential you want in a man. You can believe in him. You can have faith in him. You can see the endless possibilities in a man, but until he sees it and believes it himself and acts on it, you have nothing.

Never Chase A Man

❦

"Good men don't run. So, if you find yourself having to chase a man, stop...that's the wrong man!"

Don't Let The Hurt Fool You

"Don't ever let the hurt or the anger of a bad
separation fool you into disrespecting yourself."

Although you may have had a bad separation and feel angry at him for what he's done, never allow that anger to cause you to disrespect yourself. Some think that if they go out and are intimate with someone immediately after the breakup, they are, in some way, paying him back for what he's done; this is farthest from the truth! The truth is you are sacrificing your self-respect, dignity, and reputation as a good woman, all to try and hurt a man who's already proven he doesn't care about you. Is it really worth it? I don't think so.

Never let the actions of the wrong man cause you to lower yourself to a level that's lower than him; you are better than that. Your self-respect, dignity and your reputation, as a good woman, are far too valuable to a good man for you to throw them away trying to get revenge on the wrong man.

Bending Over Backwards

"Make sure you don't break yourself, trying to fix a man that is already broken."

There are some things you can help a man with and there are some things only he alone can fix. Don't break yourself trying to fix something that is totally outside of your power to fix. In the end, he'll still be broken and you'll end up both broken heart-ed and completely exhausted.

Why Play The Detective

"In your relationship, you should not have to play the detective to get to the truth; you should be able to ask the question and he give you the answer. It should be as simple as that."

I f it isn't, you have some big decisions to make. In my opinion, there's nothing worse than not hearing the truth from the one you love and instead, having to hear it from someone else.

When He Yells At You

"The more often he yells at you, the further you'll drift away; and then one day he'll realize that you two are so far apart emotionally, that you can't hear a word he says. By then...it's too late."

The true character of a man is not seen during the good times but during times of stress. When he yells at you, he's trying to control you or the situation. You can tell a lot about a man during these times because if he doesn't deal with it well, his true colors will begin to show. Remember, you can measure the true strength of a man by how well he controls others, but you measure his true power by how well he controls himself.

Best Friend
Vs. Boyfriend

*Just because he made a good "Best friend," doesn't
necessarily mean he'll make a good "Boyfriend."*

Theoretically, it sounds like it should work; however, it can prove to be a little more complicated. I'm not saying it can't work because I've seen it go both ways. All I am saying is you should be very careful if you are considering transitioning a current "Best friend" into the "Boyfriend" position. That switch will not only cause the expectations to change, but the rules of the relationship will change as well. If it works, great, but if it doesn't, you stand a big chance of losing both your "Boyfriend" and your "Best Friend."

The question then becomes, "are you willing to take that risk?

Trying To Convince Them Of Your Worth

❧

"Never waste your time trying to convince someone else of your worth. If they can't see it, they are not worth the effort."

The beautiful thing about the ones who truly love us is that they are always able to see our worth, even when we doubt it ourselves. In fact, they are often the ones that remind us of it whenever they think we're settling for less than what we deserve.

If you have to try to convince someone of your worth, that means they don't already know it. And if they don't already know it, how can they value you and the relationship?

Never Lose Yourself

*"Stay true to who you are as a woman. When the
relationship is in harmony with who you are, it works.
However, when it starts to make you feel like you have
to sacrifice who you are, as a woman, to make it work,
it may be time to reevaluate whether or not that
relationship is still right for you."*

Never completely lose your identity of self in a relationship. When you do, you lose your very reason for being there in the first place.

In the end, everything changes, but a healthy relationship should grow with you, not against you.

Don't Be Fooled

Don't be fooled by a man's words and his inconsistent actions. Instead, look for consistency over a long period of time because, if you think about it, every "wrong" man, that you ever dated, seemed like the "right" man in the beginning.

Take your time and be patient. Remember, dating the wrong man can be like a horror movie. In the beginning, it's always fun and exciting until the crazy one shows up. Then, things can get "real" really quick.

All I am saying is this: if you don't want to end up co-starring in his horror movie, take the time to read the script before you accept the part!

Yesterday's Happiness

"When you have to rely on yesterday's happiness in a relationship, to get you through today, it might be time to move on."

Every day is an opportunity for you to do something that adds value to your relationship and move it forward. If you are not moving forward, you're moving backward; there is no such thing as a relationship that stands still. Life is motion, and a relationship with no motion is dead.

So if there ever comes a time, in your relationship, when all you have are memories, you may need to reevaluate the relationship. Remember, memories are in the past and if that's all your relationship has, it might not have a future.

Love Means Nothing Without Loyalty

※

"A man's love for you means absolutely nothing if it doesn't come with an uncompromising loyalty to you and your relationship; that should be non-negotiable."

Without loyalty, there is not trust. Without trust, you have nothing to look forward to but headaches, heartache, and regrets. Furthermore, If you choose to give your time to a man without loyalty, just know that he will always disappoint you. It may take a little while, but sooner or later his lack of loyalty will shine through. When it does, you'll wish you had never given your time to such a man.

The Best Sex Won't Fill That Void

"The best sex in the world, without love, still won't fill that void. It's a quick fix and you won't realize it until you wake up the next morning and realize you're still alone."

Knowing What You Do And Don't Want

"Knowing what you don't want in a man is equally as important as knowing what you do want from him."

He's Not Supposed To Kill Your Dreams

"He's not supposed to make you give up on your dreams...he's supposed to help you achieve them."

Stop Grading On A Curve

"Ladies, stop grading these men on a curve. Either he meets your standards or he doesn't; stop making excuses for him!"

Lonely In A Relationship

"To be single and feel lonely is understandable, but to be in a relationship and feel lonely... that's unacceptable."

hen you are single, missing the companionship and interaction with someone you love and care about is normal. However, when you are in a relationship and still feel the same loneliness as you did when you were single, that's not normal. You have to ask yourself the following question, "Why am I even wasting my time in this relationship?"

It's possible that he may have simply gotten caught up in his day to day tasks and he may not even realize that he's caused you to feel the way you do. My advice would be for you to talk to him about how you feel and give him the opportunity to make the necessary changes.

If he does, great. If he doesn't, then maybe you need to start thinking about making some changes for yourself and your own happiness.

The Cost Of Love

They say, "Love doesn't cost a thing," but I disagree because falling in love with the wrong person could cost you everything.

For those of you who have been in a relationship where, when you finally walked away, you were physically, mentally, and emotionally exhausted; to the point where you felt like you were literally starting your life all over again, you know exactly what I mean.

For those of you who haven't experienced this feeling, when you're out there deciding who you will and who you won't give your time and ultimately your love to, just remember, your love isn't free. If you decide wrong, it could cost you everything.

CHAPTER

Seventeen

THE RIGHT MAN

"The right man won't break your heart; he'll protect it."

He Won't Want You To Lower Your Standards

*"The right man won't want you to lower your
standards; he would rather push himself
to meet or exceed them."*

Never let anyone talk you into lowering your standards! Any woman that would complain about your standards being too high has probably already compromised her own. Any man that would complain about your standards being too high is more than likely used to dealing with women who have none.

No real man takes pride in reaching a level that is easily reached. The pride comes from all the discipline and the work that we put into attaining that which others fail to achieve. The process of setting ourselves apart from the rest… that's what we live for. With love, it's no different. The right man would rather fight and earn your love and trust than for you to simply give it to him. In other words, a real man would rather not have your love at all than to get it by default.

Never compromise your standards because somewhere out there, there's a good man who is not only willing, but more than capable of meeting or exceeding them.

Pride In
Your Happiness

❧

"The right man will take pride in your happiness. He knows that the happier you are, the happier he will be."

He'll Never Judge You

"A man doesn't necessarily have to agree with your past, but he should be willing to accept it if he wants to be a part of your future."

The right man will never judge you by your past. Instead, he'll choose to respect the realness of your journey to becoming the beautiful, strong woman that you are today. He will understand that no one's perfect; however, you are the perfect culmination of all your past experiences, both the good and the bad, and with all things having been considered…he will still believe that you are perfect for him.

When You Know You Are Loved And Respected

"*His physical strength may bring you the comfort of knowing you are protected, but it's his ability to attend to your emotional needs that gives you the peace of mind that comes with knowing you are loved and respected.*"

Find your place of peace in the arms of the one that truly loves and respects you; and when you do… hold on with all your might cause you got a good man.

When The Right Man Comes Along

*"When it's the right man, you won't have to change;
he'll love you just the way you are."*

When the right man comes along, in his eyes, the most beautiful thing about you will be who you are as a woman. To him, it will be the little things you never even think about that make you so amazing.

The Right Man Will Find Strength In Unity

"The right man may disagree with you in private, but in public...he will always have your back."

The Right Man's Love

"When the right man walks into your life and loves you the way you deserve to be loved, your whole perspective on life will change."

More Than Just Your Man

✦

"The right man will want to be more to you than just your man; he'll want to be your best friend, your confidant, and the one person in this world to never disappoint you."

To the right man, it's so much bigger than just simply being your man. It's about filling in at the most important positions in your life. It's about him being the one you can confide in...the one you can talk to about anything. It's about him being the first one you come to in all your major decisions. To him, the most valuable thing in his life is being the most valuable person in yours.

He's "Ready"

❧

"The right man will find himself before
he looks for you."

Many men have sight, but only a few have a vision. Vision is what allows men to understand where we are going and what it will take to get there.

Ladies, find a man with a vision. That's the only way to be sure you two are headed for the same destination.

The Most Beautiful Things About You

"The right man will see you in a way that only a man who truly loves and adores you can see you: with his heart and not with his eyes."

The most beautiful things about you can't be seen or touched; they can't be captured in a photograph or recorded on a video. The most beautiful things about you will go unseen by the man who sees you only with his eyes and not with his heart. But the man who takes the time to really get to know you, to listen to you, and to ultimately understand you, will see you very differently. That man will see your beauty as a blind man would describe it; not based on what he sees, but based on how he feels.

You see, the right man will appreciate your beauty on the outside, but he'll love you for your beauty on the inside.

NOTES:

Describe the right man for you. The catch is, you cannot mention anything about his physical or financial assets. I want you to focus specifically on how he would meet your emotional, mental and spiritual needs.

_____

_____

_____

_____

_____

_____

_____

_____

_____

_____

_____

_____

_____

Memorize this list so that when you meet a man, regardless of his looks or his money, you can close your eyes and ask yourself whether or not he looks anything like this list. Not based on what you see, but based on how he makes you feel. If he does remind you of your list, that's a good start; but if he doesn't, you may want to reconsider whether or not he's right for you.

Part II
For Him

CHAPTER

Eighteen

FROM
ONE MAN
TO
ANOTHER

"If you love her, be strong enough, not only to tell her, but to show her as well, or be strong enough to watch her be loved by someone else."

Pay Attention To One Woman

"I believe that if some men would just stop trying to impress all women and simply focus on the physical and emotional needs of the one they are with, their lives would be far less expensive and much more fulfilling."

A man will get more fulfillment from the love of one woman than he will from the attention of many. He simply needs to focus on the woman he's with, let go of the rest and everything else will fall into place.

If You Don't Talk To Her

❦

*"If you don't talk to her, for at least an hour each day,
you'll have no idea about what is going
on in her life."*

I f you are really interested in what is going on in her life, you will take the time to talk to her and listen to what she has to say.

My advice is that you should make every effort to be a part of what's going on with her on a day to day basis. If you don't…someone else will.

Her Silence
Speaks Volumes

"A woman's silence is one of her most powerful forms
of communication; it conveys emotions, so intense, that
no words could possibly describe how she feels
at that moment."

If you find yourself on the receiving end of a woman's silent treatment and are curious as to whether or not you should be concerned, the answer is...YES!

Sometimes, all she needs is a little time. Whatever you do, don't force the issue. When you feel a break in the tension, sit down with her and talk to her about what's bothering her. Remember, don't try to justify your actions at this point. She needs you to simply listen to what she has to say. When she's finished, acknowledge her feelings and work with her to resolve the issue. It's not about winning or losing or who's right or wrong; it's about the two of you understanding and respecting each other and working together to move the relationship forward.

Talk "To" Her

Talk "to" her and not "at" her...there's a difference.

It's not always what you say, but how you say it and the tone you choose to use that often turn a simple discussion into an argument. When you talk "to" her, you are considerate of her feelings and her opinions. When you talk "at" her, you are disregarding both, and she can feel it.

My thoughts are you should never make demands. Instead, you should make requests or suggestions. Always consider getting her input on important decisions related to the relationship and even things that relate only to you. Show her that her opinion matters. Remember, your tone and how you say it will have a huge impact on how she takes it. In other words, a pleasant tone will get you a pleasant response. A negative or aggressive tone will usually get you a negative response.

For those of you who find it necessary to ask a woman how many men she's been with before you: stop asking!

For one, what does it really matter? What if she says, 2 or 10 or 20? Should what she has done in the past have any impact on how you feel about her today? If it does, maybe she would be better off finding someone who's more interested in who she is today rather than wasting her time on a man who's more concerned with who she was five years ago. Besides, to be honest, it's a question that most of us expect women to answer honestly, but if we were asked the same, we would have a difficult time giving her an honest answer.

In the end, it's the past! If you love her, accept all of her, including all the past life experiences that have contributed to making her the woman she is today: both the good and the bad.

Be Honest About Your Intentions

❧

"A woman needs a man to be honest and upfront with her, from the beginning, about his intentions. Don't let months, or even years go by before you finally get the courage to tell her you're not ready to commit."

Don't take away her ability to decide what's best for her by lying about your true intentions. Just be honest. Some women are open to different types of relationships, whether it involves a commitment or not. All I'm saying is be upfront and honest with her. She has a right to choose what's best for her.

The Old You

*If a woman ever says, "I miss the old you," that is a
warning to let you know that you've changed
and not in a good way.*

Sometimes we as men don't pay enough attention to the warning signs until it's too late. Comments like, "you used to do that for me all the time, how come you don't do it anymore" or "I really miss when we used to..." should be a red flag. These, among others, are not just empty comments; these comments say that she is beginning to look to the past portion of the relationship for her happiness, instead of the present.

My thoughts...pay attention to these comments and try to reincorporate whatever it is she's asking for into your current plans. If for no other reason, do it because it makes her happy.

Boredom

There are a lot of reasons why a woman could lose interest in a man... "BOREDOM" is one of them.

When a woman says she wants consistency, she doesn't mean she wants you to do the "same thing" over and over. For her, love is a new and exciting experience. She wants you to be consistent but creative. She wants you to bring stability, while at the same time being able to be spontaneous and willing to try new and exciting things with her.

I've heard many women say they look forward to spending every moment they can with the man they love. That's because they understand that those moments, if spent with the right man, have the potential of later becoming great memories.

So, for the men reading this, don't be afraid to try something different: surprise her. It doesn't have to be something big. In fact, the best memories are often made from the smaller things. Whatever you do, be consistent with your love and creative in how you show it.

Check Your Ego

"Don't lose her because you allow your ego to become bigger than your heart."

Winning isn't everything, especially when you're in a relationship and the loser is going to be the woman you love. Don't let your ego cause you to push an issue with her that, in the end, gains you nothing but a boost to your ego. As a result, you've damaged your relationship with her. I have a saying I go by and it states simply this, "When in a relationship, never let your ego write a check that only a single man can cash."

To Hear The Truth From You

❧

"Everyone makes mistakes. She knows you're not perfect, and she doesn't expect you to be. But when it comes to the truth, she would much rather hear it from you than to be blindsided and hear it from someone else."

When She Talks To You

❧

"When she shares with you her problems, it's not that she's complaining; she simply trusts you enough to talk to you about them."

For her to open up to you and share with you both the good and bad, is one of the greatest compliments she could give to you. It says that she trusts you and respects your opinion. Even more, it says that she feels comfortable talking to you and that there's no one else she would rather share her feelings with than you.

Spend Time, Not Money

❧

"Making a good woman feel secure in the relationship has nothing to do with how much money you spend ON HER, but rather how much quality time you are willing to spend WITH HER."

A good woman is not interested in your Money or your status. What she wants from you is your time, loyalty, love, commitment and for you to treat her like nothing else in the world matters.

Overreacting

There is no such thing as her "overreacting." The reaction is a direct reflection of how she felt at that very moment.

For you to say to her, "you are overreacting" or "you're being too emotional" is to totally disregard her emotional state at that moment. The reality is that she is most likely responding to something that has been building up inside, for some time, and whatever just occurred was her breaking point. Instead of criticizing or disregarding her feelings, you should acknowledge them. Sit down and talk with her so that together, you two can resolve the underlying issue. If you don't, the issue will not go away…it will only get worse.

Just Because She Smiles

"Just because she smiles, doesn't mean she's happy. To understand how she really feels, you have to let her talk and you have to be willing to listen."

Time Vs. Quality Time

When she says "spend time" with her, she is actually saying she wants you to spend "quality time" with her. She doesn't always say "quality" because she figures that should go without saying.

S pending time means more to her than simply you two being in the same house or room at the same time; it means engaging her on a physical, mental, and emotional plane as well. Sometimes, we think just because we share the same physical space, we are "spending time" when in fact, if you are in the same room with her and not engaging her on some level, you're wasting time.

True Value Of Love

"True value is found in the love of a good woman, not material things. The most valuable thing that you, as a man, could ever have is not your watch, car or your house, it's the real love of the good woman sitting there right next to you. The one who would still love you and be on your side, even if you lost all those material things tomorrow."

A good woman's love is always loyal. When was the last time money was loyal to you?

When She Says, "I'm Okay"

When she says, "I'm okay" it doesn't necessarily mean that she's okay. You have to really get to know her to understand her and know the difference.

You have to learn to speak her language. You have to learn to sometimes bypass her words and feel the vibe she's giving you. That is what will tell you whether or not things are truly "okay" or not. If they are, great; but if they're not, talk to her. Don't let too much time pass without finding out what's on her mind. If you do, things may just get worse.

She's Not Stupid

❧

*"She's not stupid! Don't try to play her like she is.
You're insulting her intelligence. If you're not careful,
you'll one day find yourself on the outside wishing
you could get back in."*

If You Are Cheating
...She Knows

❧

*"If you're cheating and you think she doesn't know...she
knows. She may not have enough evidence to prove it
right now, but deep down inside, she knows; Her
intuition is foolproof. It's only a
matter of time now."*

CHAPTER
Nineteen

SHE HAS HER LIMITS

"A good woman's love is powerful. Some of you have a good woman and will never experience the true power of her love because your inconsistencies prevent her from being able to fully love you the way she wants to."

She's Willing To Fight For You

"A good woman is willing to fight long and hard for the man she loves and believes in; but just because she's willing to fight for you, doesn't mean she won't leave you, if you take her loyalty for granted."

When You Change

"When a good woman leaves, it's usually not because of another man; but rather because you've changed and the man you've become, is no longer the same as the one she fell in love with."

Inconsistent Love

"*If your love isn't consistent, She will perceive it to be non-existent.*"

She Would Rather Let Go

"*She would rather let go of you altogether than to try and hold on to bits and pieces of a relationship that you're no longer committed to.*"

She Can't Talk To You

*"One of the biggest mistakes you could make is to cause
the woman you love to feel like she can't talk to you."*

Once she feels like she can't communicate with you, she becomes frustrated. That frustration will slowly turn into anger and resentment. The little things then become the big things. Before you know it, you're arguing over something that, to you, seems small; but to her, it's not the one thing, it's the combination of all the things she feels like she can't talk to you about.

My thoughts...take the time to, not only listen to her, but encourage her to talk to you about everything. You don't always have to agree with her, but you should always be willing to listen to her.

In the end, that's one of your responsibilities as her man; if she can't talk to you, then who?

You Can't Be Mad

*You can't be mad at her for leaving when you are the
one who pushed her away. What was she supposed to
do? No matter how strong she is, there's only so much
she can take before she finally says, "Enough!"*

A good woman doesn't leave the man she loves for
another man; she leaves because she is unhappy,
and she feels as if leaving is the only option she
has left.

She's tired of trying to talk about things with a man
who refuses to listen. She's tired of being ignored and
treated like her feelings don't matter. She's tired of feeling
like the only time she can get any affection, from the man
she loves, is during sex...she's tired. All she wants is for
you to love her and treat her like she matters.

If you really and truly love her, don't push her away.
All I ask is that you put your pride aside, for a moment,
and just think about it.

Hard For Her To Walk Away

"It's never easy."

It's never easy for a good woman to walk away; especially after she's invested so much of herself into making it work. Just know, that by the time she finally decides to leave, she's given you countless chances and debated the idea, over and over in her head, at least 1000 times. She's exhausted; she's frustrated and totally heartbroken to have to walk away from a man who, deep down inside, she still loves and is still willing to fight for.

Often she will leave the door slightly open, for a short period, in hopes that you will come around, but if you wait too long…she'll be gone forever.

NOTES:

List 5 things that you think were contributing factors to your past relationships not working out.

1. _____

2. _____

3. _____

4. _____

5. _____

Now, take a step back and ask yourself what role, if any, your actions or inactions may have played in causing the above relationship to fail.

_____

_____

Finally, write down how you are going to change those things so that your current or future relationships have a better chance of succeeding and they don't end with the same results as your past relationships.

_____

_____

_____

_____

_____

_____

_____

_____

_____

CHAPTER

WHAT SHE WANTS...
WHAT SHE NEEDS...

*"She wants to give in to you; mind, body, and soul.
All she needs from you is the assurance that you
won't make her regret it in the end."*

How Can You Blame Her?

*"She's been lied to, cheated on and had her heart bro-
ken by a man she'd given years of her life to. He stepped
on her love, violated her trust and disrespected her.
After all that, who can blame her for questioning the
intentions of a man she just met?"*

Too often, we as men complain about how wom-
en bring the results of a past broken heart into
their new relationships. My question is, who
can blame her?

I believe, as a whole, too many of us look at the problem from the wrong perspective. We spend all our time
complaining about the results and ignore the fact that
our actions, as men, are largely responsible for creating
the results in the first place. Remember, it's cause first

and then effect, not the other way around. If we want women to change then we have to give them a better past experience to pull from; we have to stop acting like none of this is our fault, accept responsibility for it and change it.

She's Looking For Your Patience And Understanding

"She doesn't blame you. She's looking for you to change her whole experience and give her a reason to love one more time."

She's a good woman who has had her heart broken over and over by the men she's loved in the past. She has a right to be frustrated and upset. Don't minimize her pain. When you do, she feels even more frustrated that you don't understand all that she's been through and how she feels. Remember, she's not looking for your sympathy, she's looking for your patience and understanding.

She Needs A Man Who Is Not Afraid

*She needs a man who is not afraid to give himself
completely to her without fear of consequence
and without pause.
A man not afraid to allow himself to become
emotionally vulnerable in order to make that
deep connection she so needs.
A love connection so deep that it sits at the very
footsteps of her soul.
Now, I'm not talking about an ordinary love,
I'm talking about that next level type of love;
That type of love that only fairytale books speak of.
That's what she wants...that's what she needs.*

More Than Just Her Man

She needs you to be more than just her man.
She needs you to be her best friend and her confidant;
for you to be her voice of reason, when she needs advice,
and her soundboard when she needs to vent.
At the end of the day, she needs you to be the one person
who, no matter how terrible the storm,
she can always count on to protect her from the rain.
She needs all of this to be consistent,
something she can count on to never change.
That's what she wants...that's what she needs.

Defend Her Honor

"A woman wants a man that she knows will step up to defend her honor, regardless of the consequences, whether she's there or not to defend herself."

She Needs A

Strong Man

"A strong woman doesn't need a man to take care of her. What she needs is a man secure enough to understand that and not be intimidated by it."

Value Her Opinion

"She wants a man who respects and values her opinion; a man she feels comfortable enough to be able to disagree with without the fear of it always turning into a full-blown argument."

Talk About Anything And Everything

"She wants a man she can talk to about anything and everything because she feels just that comfortable with him."

She Wants
Your Attention

"She wants the attention from you, her man, not a stranger; a simple compliment from you, at the right time, could change her whole day."

She knows when it comes from you, it's out of love; but when it comes from a stranger, it's more often than not, out of lust.

With that in mind, take every opportunity to put a smile on the face of the woman you love. After all, what greater feeling is there than to know that she is happy and smiling, and you're the reason for it.

She'd Rather Hear Your Voice

"She would much rather hear your voice
than read your text."

It's not the words you speak, but the emotions you convey through your speed, tone, and style that give her insight into your sincerity.

In her mind, the words "I love you" or "I miss you" may look good in a text, but when she hears you say them and your actions support it...it simply feels good.

Be Different Than Her Ex

Don't try to be "better" than her ex, be "different" from
her ex. She's tired of the same old thing.
She's ready for you to show her something different.

The competition is over: you won. If she wanted more of what he had to offer, she would have gone back to him, but instead, she chose you. Don't give her more of the same thing. Create a whole new lane and show her something different.

Notice The Small Things

"When you don't take the time to notice the little things, such as her new hair style, or her new nail color or outfit, she not only notices, but she makes a mental note of the fact that you didn't notice as well."

Pay attention to the little things that she does and don't be afraid to compliment her. You may think that she won't notice or that it doesn't matter but it does. She cares about your opinion. Plus, she does these things, not only for herself, but at times, for you as well.

At every chance, let her know how beautiful she is and that you truly appreciate her.

Challenge Her

*"Challenge her to be the best she can be. Sometimes,
just knowing you support her is all the extra
push she needs."*

Y ou, being her man and one of the most important people in her life right now, your support
means a lot to her. She looks to you to challenge
her and support her every step of the way. If she can't
count on you, then who? You have to understand that
she may get frustrated at times and say that she doesn't
need your help. She may also tell you that she can do it
all on her own, and that may be true too, but at the end
of the day, you're her man and because she has you…she
shouldn't have to.

Keep Her Close

⸻❦⸻

"Pay attention to her. Talk to her. Listen to her. Love her. Respect her. Keep her so close that you leave no room for her to doubt."

Doubt comes from there being distance between the two of you; whether that distance is in a physical, mental or emotional form, the result can be very stressful on your relationship. The man that understands this will do everything in his power to keep her close, leaving her no room to doubt his love for her and his uncompromising loyalty and commitment to her and the relationship.

Love Is Not About "Cuffing" For A Season

Real love is not about "cuffing" her for a season. It's about setting her heart free to love and trust you without the fear of consequences for a lifetime.

To remove her fears, you have to make her feel secure in the relationship. To make it last a lifetime, you have to be willing to commit to her. That's the type of love a good man gives...that's the type of love a good woman needs.

Make It Believable

"Simply telling her you love her is not enough, you have to consistently show her as well. It's the combination of the two that makes it believable."

When you only say that you love her, she still has questions because she hears it, but she never sees it. When you only show her that you love her, she still has questions because she sees it, but she never hears it. However, when you tell her that you love her, and you show her as well, she not only sees it and hears it, but she now feels it. And the feeling of being truly loved, is what makes it believable.

Take Her Breath Away

That's what she wants...that's what she needs.
You see, she needs a man that can take her breath away
and make it hard for her to breathe.
She needs a man that makes her feel so weak
that she drops down to her knees;
but not for the reason you think.
You see, even the wrong man can catch her eye, but only
the right man can capture her imagination
and stimulate her mind.
So when she drops down to her knees, it's to thank God
for his hand,
in putting her in the right place, at the right time,
to meet the right man.
That's all she ever wanted....that's all she ever needed.

What Are Her Dreams

❦

What are her dreams and ambitions?
Have you asked her?
If not, why?
That's a big part of being her man.
How can you support what you don't know?

Part III
For Both Of You

CHAPTER

Twenty-One

MAKING IT WORK

*"When the love is real, you won't have to
find time for each other...
you'll make time."*

Part Of The Solution

*"It's hard for either of you to help find a solution when
you both refuse to recognize that your actions or
inactions may be a part of the problem."*

It's a lot easier for you to blame each other, for all of
the problems in the relationship, than to accept the
fact that your actions or inactions may have caused
at least some of the problems in the first place. This goes
both ways. In order for you to be able to find viable
solutions to any problem, you both have to be willing
to accept the fact that you, yourself, may be a part of the
problem to begin with. If you both take this approach
and are honest with yourselves and each other, your dis-
cussions, which previously would have turned into arguments, should become more productive. That's because
you will have shifted from a "blame" based way of thinking to a more "solution" based way of thinking.

Remember, the goal of the discussion is not for either

person to win. The goal is to find a solution that works for both of you and allows your relationship to move forward in a positive direction.

Arguments Don't Solve Anything

"Arguments don't solve anything. The louder you get, the less the other person listens; in the end, you may think you have won...but at what cost?"

Don't risk your happiness over something that means nothing more to you than a personal stroke to your ego. Remember, you two are on the same team. That means if one of you lose, you both lose. You can minimize your arguments by not playing the "blame game." If there's a problem, look for a solution that is in the best interest of the relationship.

Don't Make Rules That You Won't Follow

"Stop making rules, in your relationship, that you expect them to follow, but you are unwilling to follow yourself."

I f there are going to be rules, then the rules should be agreed upon and equally applied. If one or more rules are going to be applied differently, then both of you should agree to it (not just one of you). No one person in a relationship should have privilege over the other; it's a partnership, not a dictatorship. I know they say that life isn't always fair, but in my opinion, your relationship should always try to be.

Don't Become A Stranger

"When was the last time you two just sat down and talked? Don't let the one you love become a stranger... make time for each other today."

Often times we become so wrapped up in our day-to-day activities that we forget to just sit down and talk to the ones we love. There are some people out there, right now, who are at the point where they walk in and out of rooms without speaking to each other; they pass each other in the hallway as if the other person doesn't even exist, and they sleep in the same bed physically, but emotionally, they're separated.

Don't ever let this become you. Always make time for each other.

The Magic Is In Your Presence

"Take time to make time for each other."

They say that absence makes the heart grow fonder, but I believe that absence makes two hearts grow apart. Remember how you fell in love; it wasn't all the time you spent away from each other that caused you to feel the way you do, but rather those powerful moments that you spent together.

When it comes to love, the magic is found in the presence, not the absence. Too much of an absence and the magic begins to fade away.

Healthy Relationship

"Healthy, strong relationships are based upon building up, not tearing down."

For a relationship to survive, both of you need to feel like you have an equal say in matters and that your opinion counts. For one of you to tear the other down with verbal abuse, physical abuse or other methods of intimidation, serves no other purpose but to weaken the unit as a whole. This will ultimately destroy your relationship.

Instead of tearing each other down, focus on ways to build each other up; support and encourage each other through both words and actions. The goal should be to grow stronger every day as a couple. Actively take time to focus on this. Act as if you were being watched every day and that you would receive a grade on your performance at the end of each day. It's a fact that when you focus on certain things, you perform better at those things than when you don't focus on them. I know it sounds like a lot of work, but trust me, once you've changed your way of thinking, and it becomes a habit, it will get easier. In the end, your relationship will continue to grow without limits! So today...let's focus!

Nothing Comes Between You

❦

"As long as you love him and he loves you and you both are fully committed to making it work, nothing or no one can ever come between you."

That's the true power of mutual love and commitment. It creates an impenetrable circle of love that can't be broken from the outside... only from the inside.

Talking About Anything

"If you two can talk to each other openly and honestly about anything and everything, you two can get through anything and everything."

Strength Of Your Relationship

"When things get hard, don't just give up without trying; it's those hard times that often help define the true strength of the relationship."

CHAPTER

Twenty-Two

LOVE

*"Make her smile. Make her laugh.
Make her feel so beautiful that all she wants
to do is hold you in her arms and dance all night."*

What Does Love Mean To You

Love is probably one of the most powerful and mis-used word in our vocabulary. If you ask 100 different people what love means to them, you would probably get 100 different answers. Here's my take: love is the indescribable way someone makes you feel inside. It's a feeling that grips you at the very core of your soul; one that makes you feel like nothing else. For a woman, it's comforting, reassuring and provides her with a sense of peace and security. For a man, it strengthens our resolve, gives us a sense of purpose, and the confidence to believe we can accomplish anything.

I F I were one of 100 asked, that would be my answer. Different people equate love with many different things. Some equate it with money while others may equate it to something else. I'm not here to say which is right or wrong nor am I here trying to judge anyone. All I ask is that you take a moment and ask yourself what love means to you. Once you have your answer, you'll know exactly what kind of love you'd be willing to accept from someone else.

A Good Woman's True Love

"When a woman truly loves a man, the only person who can mess that up is that man himself."

A woman's true love for man is foolproof; she'll be with her man, side-by-side with her man through anything and everything. If that ever changes, it's most often based on something he did or did not do because no one else has that power; not her friends, not her family...no one. No one has the power to change a woman's true love for her man except the man she truly loves.

Give Her 100% Or Nothing At All

"If you are going to love her, give her 100% or nothing at all. Anything less and you are, not only cheating her, but you are cheating yourself as well."

She Still Believes

"If she decides to give you a second chance, it's usually not because you deserve it; but rather because she still believes in you and the idea that love, if given the chance, will somehow prevail in the end."

Dear Love

"Dear love,
you are her greatest addiction,
one for which she desires no cure.
And she will never need rehab
as long as you keep it 100% pure."

A woman's greatest addiction is not her shoes, handbags, or shopping, but rather it's the feeling she gets when she knows she's truly loved; that is…her greatest addiction of all.

Old Way To Love

With all the new and improved ways to do things in the world today, she still prefers your love the old-fashioned way. She doesn't mind reading your texts, but she would much rather hear your voice. It's okay to FaceTime, but she would much rather spend quality time with you. To be honest, she wants you to be so up close and personal with her that you leave no room for anything to come between the two of you...

not even technology.

Letting Go Of Everything

"You have to be willing to let go of everything to be able to hold each other forever."

Holding Hands

Call it being old-fashioned, but she still loves it when you hold her hand. There's just something about that physical connection that really does it for her. Somehow, it allows you to speak to her spirit and say in a firm, yet gentle voice, "Relax, you don't have to worry about anything...I got you."

Hand Written Love Letters

"Handwritten love letters; the rare jewel of the past that somehow was able to convey emotions that today's text message cannot."

There's just something about being able to pour your feelings out in a hand-written letter that adds something more to it than simply typing it out in a text message. Maybe, it's the time spent; who knows. All I know is that reading a letter, that was written by the one you love, just feels different. You should try it. You never know, you might just discover something incredible about each other.

Grandparents Style Of Love

❧

Think about it for a second...they didn't have any email, cell phones, text messages, Twitter, Facebook, or Instagram and they made it work. Not because it was easier, but because, back then, they had to spend quality time with each other because there was no other way to make it work. Maybe that's a lesson from the past that we can all learn from.
Take time to spend time...it works.

Appreciate Her

"Appreciate the beautiful woman she is and never let
her fall asleep without knowing that she is
truly loved and adored by you."

The Journey Of Love

"Love is less about the destination and more about the
beauty of the journey...make it unforgettable."

CHAPTER

Twenty-Three

PASSION
AND
ROMANCE

"Good company, good conversation, a nicely dim lit
room, soft music and a glass of something smooth
is all she needs right now."

Something Different 1

She wants you to burn candles that are scented;
She wants rose petals at her feet as she walks down the
hallway of passion to ecstasy...
She wants you to show her something different.
She wants to hear a different song
with a little more beat to it.
She wants you to, not only kiss it,
but to speak to it...
She wants you to show her something different.
She wants you to make love,
not only to her body, but her mind too.
She wants to feel the anticipation
before you slide through.
She wants you to change everything
she's ever been used to...
She wants you to show her something different.

Something Different 2

That's what she wants...that's what she needs.
You see, she wants you to walk into that bedroom
wearing all black everything.
While she stands there in the middle of the room
wearing that sexy black dress
and those sexy black heels,
she wants you to grab her around the waist,
pin her back against the wall and let her know
it's about to get real.
You see, passion speaks louder than words
and all that nonsense she's already heard...
She's ready for you to show her something different.

Watch You Sleep

He just wants to watch you sleep.
As you lie there in the bed next to him
with your eyes closed and your beautiful body
still holding the scent from the bath full of roses...
He just wants to watch you sleep.
For you to lay your head on his chest and let the
warmth of your breath breathe fire into his soul.
I don't think you'll ever know just how good it feels for
him to simply just be there...
to watch you sleep.

Real Love And Real Passion

She needs real love and real passion.
That type of love and passion
that goes beyond the fathoms of what her mind
and body can even imagine...
That's what she needs.
You see,
she needs to feel the sensation
of a strong man's internal heat,
for it to burn deep down into her soul
in a place where only heaven and earth meet...
That's what she needs.
She needs a bold man with a fire for passion,
one that believes in taking control
and don't believe in asking...
That's what she needs.

Not Intimidated
By Her Sexuality

She needs a man that's not intimidated
by her sexuality.
A man that's not afraid to explore her fantasies
and make them her reality.
You see, a grown woman has her own visions
and an insecure man can make her feel like she's
locked in a prison. But a secure man,
he'll set her mind and body free;
free to be anything she wants to be
without fear of being judged.
Free to be a woman in the day and a freak in the dark,
all in the name of love...
That's what she needs.

Walk With Her

Take a walk with her.
Find an intimate place where the ambiance
is so beautiful that it can never be erased from her
mind, body, or her soul;
Take a walk with her and just talk.
The power of you walking and holding her hand,
next to a restless ocean as it crashes down
and erases the footsteps in the sand is unforgettable;
Just walk with her.
You'll learn more about her during that walk
than you could have ever learned during a thousand
movies or a thousand meals.
You'll learn about her dreams, her passions, and her
pains that she may or may not conceal;
Just walk with her.

When The Day Is Finally Over

When the day is finally over,
she wants you to make time to change
her view of the world.
She wants you to dim the lights, play her favorite song
and sit there talking and laughing
about whatever is going on in her life.
She wants to finally fall asleep in your arms.
She wants you to grab the wine glass from her hand,
then stand and gently pick her up
and carry her off to a far away land,
where the beds are made of gold and the floors
are made of sand.
You see, it's not that hard to understand, that at the
end of the day, all she wants is to spend that quality
time with you, her man.

"Take her somewhere she's never been;
Show her something she's never seen,
and make her feel like she's never felt."

-Mr. Amari Soul

Part IV
My Private Collection

CHAPTER

PERSONAL
THOUGHTS

You Deserve Better Than Me

When I look at you,
I still see all the pain I put you through.
The make-up on your eyes can't hide the pain you feel
inside...I know.
If I could change the past I would.
I'd take it all back if I could...
You deserve so much better than me.

All your friends would say I was wrong
for leading you on like I was ready to commit,
while knowing deep down inside,
I was still on that nonsense.
I was a young man playing a young boy's game,
such a selfish thing...
You deserve so much better than me.

If I were you I would be
packing all my things and leaving them in the middle of the street.
I would have done it in a heartbeat
because you deserve so much better than me.

How I would justify in my mind,
staying out all night.
I would tell myself "I'm the man"
and that was supposed to make it right.
As you waited faithfully for me to come home,
I was in her bed doing wrong...
You deserve so much better than me.

So today, I apologize
for all those sleepless nights.
I guess I can't get mad when I see, you and him in the streets
because you finally found better than me.

She Knows
And Now I Know

She knows what it's like to be cheated on;
to feel that pain in her chest that makes it
hard for her to breathe.
She knows what it's like to get that knot in her stomach
that makes it hard for her to eat...she knows.
She knows what it's like to cry herself to sleep;
She knows what it's like to want to lock herself in her
bedroom for weeks...she knows.
And after all those years of being less than a man it
pains me to think,
that somewhere in my past she existed
and she felt this way because of me.

Bound By The Limits

Dear love,
I've been bound by the limits of a man's mind.
Shackled by the chauvinistic ideals of the man's time.
And now... I search passionately for a better place;
a place far beyond the past that cannot be
forgotten or erased.
So I ask of you...
Dear Love, if by chance you possessed the key,
I would be your slave forever,
if you would just set me free.

My Fears

*As a man, I used to sometimes do things
that seemed counter productive to my
relationship's growth. I would pull away; I created
problems where there were none and I would argue
over small things that really meant nothing to me.
I guess you could say that you and I were somewhat the
same. In the end, the closer we got,
the more afraid we became.
I never understood until I began to actually listen to
you. That's when I realized...
I was just as afraid of being hurt as you were.*

Who Am I

Who am I?
I am but a knight in his shining armor;
Young & Restless though without the drama.
I am that spark which ignites the flames;
one that continuously burns even when it rains
inside your mind, body and soul, though I know, that
even small fires can lose control. As we grow,
keep in mind as our spirits combine
and your heart beats in tune with mine;
I'm just a mere man in this land who's trying
to leave a memorable impression in the sands of time...
Who Am I?

A New Day
A New Prayer

I used to pray and ask God to send me a good woman
until I realized I was doing it all wrong...
so I changed it. Now when I pray, I don't simply ask
that he send me a good woman, but I ask that he bless
me with all the insight, patience and understanding
that I will need to make a good woman want to stay.

Angel Of Mine

I had a dream last night.
In my dream, I was approached by a woman.
I couldn't see her face, but she had the most beautiful set
of wings that I had ever seen.
Her voice...as soft and warm
as a gentle summer breeze.
I became lost in her presence...
Even more so, I became consumed by her very essence.
This is what she said to me, "To the man I love, I'd be
willing to give you the wings off my back if it would
help you to fly. All I ask is that you love me."

The Unwritten Love Letter

To my love,
You are the most beautiful being
that I have ever seen in my entire life.
And no dream will ever compare
to the reality that we share
or the passion on this moonlit night.
Now as for you, follow your dreams
when you see your vision is clear,
and worry not about companionship for I will always
be near. I am your friend, indeed, one whom you can
depend on when in need; I'll be your breath when you
cannot breathe...I'll be all you'll ever need.
Through the good times and the bad,
through the happy times and the sad,
though I'll sometimes make you mad...I'll be the best
friend you've ever had.

Compliments

Note to self... My woman is not a mind reader.

She spends an hour or more getting ready before we leave. She pays close attention to every detail, from the highlights in her hair to the shade she chooses for her nail color. I see she's wearing that new dress, and I must admit, I love the way it brings out the color in her eyes. Those shoes, I know they're her favorite by the way she stands and smiles in front of the full body mirror right before we walk out the door. I also know that she only wears them if she knows she won't be standing long because they hurt her feet. I must say though, I do love the way they add several inches to her height and the way they accent her calve muscles. I know I don't always say it, but I think it all the time. So today, I'm saying this as a friendly reminder to myself, as well as to everyone else who finds themselves forgetting this important fact: our women are not mind readers. Don't let one more second pass without letting her know just how beautiful and amazing she is.

Mac Or
Maybelline

*It's not the Mac or the Maybelline
that I see in my dreams,
but it's the beautiful face that lies beneath it.
It's not the eyeliner or the blush that makes me feel like
a young boy with a crush... it's you.
It's that beautiful woman first thing in the morning
before you do what you do...it's you.
Every day you wear that mask
for the rest of the world to see,
but every morning I feel blessed because you've
saved your natural beauty just for me.*

Something You Aint Used To

I want to sneak up from behind you and grab you by the waistline and slowly guide you back towards me. I want you to lean your head back and close your eyes and be open to whatever comes to mind. You see, I'm not afraid to color outside the lines and change every thing you've ever been used to. You would think I'd be trying to bump and grind, like those other guys, cause that's something that you're used to. You would think that I'd be trying to run my hands along your inner thighs, cause that's something that you're used to. But I'm not trying to bump and grind nor am I trying to run my hands along your inner thighs, baby I'm just trying to get inside your mind cause that's something you ain't used to.

I Know Your Secret

*Most men, if you ask them
what is the most sensitive part of a woman's body,
they'll most likely reply, "Her breasts, her neck,
her ear or maybe even her inner thigh."
I've realized that it's not your breasts, your neck, your
ear or your inner thigh...it's your mind.
So, if a man wants to really take you to that next level,
he'll need to start there hours before he even touches
you. To put it simply, it's not just about the physical;
it's about creating an emotional experience that should
take you to a place where passions explode like
fireworks in your mind leaving you physically and
emotionally exhausted from the journey. Some may
agree while others may not, but only those who have
been there truly know.*

Breathe

I want to exhale your past;
So I can inhale your presence
and breathe life into our future.

The Mystery Of You

I want to enjoy the mystery of not knowing you.
Take in every exciting opportunity to learn you.
Then, fall in love with the anticipation
of one day truly understanding you,
so that I can become totally obsessed
with the beauty of doing all the things
that make you smile.

My Favorite Story

"It's not the cover of a book that makes it a keeper...it's the story."

If you were a book, I would describe you as one with a most beautiful cover.
One that was so sexy and unique that it stood out from all the others.
Now, that may be enough for me to pick you up and peruse your pages
because relationships are like an open book,
and the intro is the first of several stages.
But, to be honest, I need more than just a pretty cover for me to keep you.
I need to fall in love with your story
and you have to promise to fit me into your sequel.

To all of you good men who are actively looking to improve your relationship and are truly dedicated to learning and understanding everything there is to know about meeting the emotional needs of the woman in your life, I salute you.

I Salute You

She's searched for so long, and it hasn't been easy. She's been let down, lied to and had her heart broken along the way. If you ask her, she'll tell you she'd almost all but given up on love. And then one day, you showed up. You gave to her what she had spent many nights praying for: The feeling of being loved, respected, challenged, supported and the emotional security that could only come from your unwavering commitment to her and the relationship. And now, not only does she believe in true love again, but she believes in you. Though her journey has been hard, I'd be willing to bet that she'd do it all over again if it would lead her back into your arms.

My friend, I salute you, from one man to another, for being the exception and not the rule...for being a good man to a good woman and changing her whole perspective on life and love.

Acknowledgments

I want to take this opportunity to first thank God for giving me the strength and the insight to write this book.

I'd like to thank my mother for being my greatest example of what a good woman is. You always have been and always will be my greatest inspiration. To my father, thank you for continuing to provide me with invaluable knowledge and wisdom. I've never known another man like you. Everyone has a hero...you will always be mine.

To all my family and friends who had a part in helping me to create this book, thank you for all your support and your encouraging words. I could not have done it without you.

Lastly, thank you to my extended social media family on Twitter, Instagram, Facebook and Pinterest. Every day I am inspired by your stories to continue writing in hopes that together, we can change the world, one heart at a time. Again, thank you all.

Please leave a review at your place of purchase.

CPSIA information can be obtained
at www.ICGtesting.com
Printed in the USA
LVOW12s0247150616
492671LV00001B/8/P